Who'd Be A Teacher?

COLOURFUL LANGUAGE

Marcus Owen

First Edition 2015

Thanks...

To all those who support my work through buying my books or sharing my stuff online.

A nod to the National Union of Teachers and to the many teacher oriented web pages who try to create solidarity and an atmosphere of support.

Thanks to Keith Hatton for many words of wisdom and Mike Whale of the NUT for his support.

Thanks also to former UK Secretary for Education, Michael Gove, whose constant interference has been truly inspiring !

Oh No. Not Another One!

This my second 'Who'd Be A Teacher?' book, so welcome back if you already have the first one!

And if not..why not?
Go on. Go buy one. It's great.
I can wait here until you get back..

Ready? Ok. Why another book?

Well, it's mainly because I have enough content for one. Since the first book, I have continued to produce cartoons to post online, some to support digital protests and some to promote my work. I am regularly inspired/ incensed by the nonsense that the teaching profession has to suffer.
I also wanted to produce a colour version this time around. The 'prequel' was entirely black and white, as that was how I had originally drawn my sketches. I didn't think to work in colour until I started digitally enhancing my line drawings for use online.

These have proved very popular and so here we have a collection of those pictures, as well as a few not having ever graced the internet. So this is a hard copy but in paperback, which is almost an oxymoron. Unlike 'relaxed observation', which definitely is!

I have also indulged myself in writing a few bits and pieces, all based upon real experiences, mine or other people's. These are observations/ recollections that wouldn't work too well as a single cartoon or would require a comic strip to express otherwise.

So there you also have the rationale for the sub-title, 'Colourful Language'. It has colour and it uses more language. Not subtle I know, but it was either that or 'School Wars- The Inspector Strikes Back'.

I'll make a similar disclaimer to last time that no real person is deliberately shown here, and any passing resemblance is pure chance. Anyone referenced in recollections is obscured by anonymity and small factual changes. I am not likely to waste time immortalising people I don't like in word or picture, as much as they may wish it!

Also, my cartoons deal with generalisations, but that doesn't necessarily mean by drawing an idiot parent, an awful headteacher or an evil school inspector that I think all parents are idiots or all headteachers are awful...

Hope you enjoy.

M.

(Please note that to provide a cheaper alternative to this full colour version, the same content is released in black and white as 'Who'd Be A Teacher?- Seeing it in Black and White.')

CONTENTS

Grumble
While
You
Work...

You've kept them in their seats all day.
You've motivated the disinterested.
You've enthused the lethargic.
You've withstood the invasive drop-ins.
You've tolerated the criticisms.
You've responded to the very latest initiatives.
You're shattered.

Don't listen to what anyone says.
That's outstanding.

Scapegoat : Innocent animal blamed for other people's mistakes...

In Modern Times

Teacher : Much the same really...

THE BAD SCHOOL DICTIONARY

unprofessional [uhn-pruh-fesh-uh-nl]

adjective : any activity not done to the particular satisfaction of the headteacher, any response that disagrees with anything the headteacher decides

noun : a person who occasionally can be described as behaving in the above manner

union representative : [yoon-yuh n rep-ri-zen-tuh-tiv]

noun : a divisive stirrer, unprofessional (see above)

teaching assistant : [tee-ching uh-sis-tuh nt]

noun : someone to exploit when you don't want to pay for a teacher

work / life balance : [wurk lahyf bal-uh ns]

noun : a state of equilibrium or equipoise; equal distribution of work and leisure / family life, a nuisance and obstacle to school plans

8

'Look at that!
Sloping off
at four o'clock.'

AND WHAT EXACTLY DO
YOU THINK HE IS GOING TO
DO WHEN HE GETS HOME?

She was amazed at the depths she had to sink to in order to find a decent school. The class were a bit wet, with memories like goldfish, but she soon got used to the pressure...

The "Ideal" Oath?

DEFINITIVE ACRONYMS FOR TEACHING (D.A.F.T)

Oh, how we love labelling our learning objectives with 'We Are Learning To', (W.A.L.T.) and 'What I'm Looking For', (W.I.L.F) Those essential acronyms should be displayed for any successful observation. Their very presence can apparently define if you are a good teacher or not. Here are some other more useful examples...

When you are asked about a child you may have overlooked in this lesson, always rely on the 'Learner's Individual Education Scheme.' (L.I.E.S.)

Due to constant 'innovations' across the curriculum, most schools now have a School Teachers Retraining Every Single Subject policy. (S.T.R.E.S.S.)

A collective body of Parents Regularly Abusing Teaching Staff are known as the P.R.A.T.S.

Also, the true meaning of O.F.S.T.E.D. is of course Originally Failed School Teacher, Ensuring Despair.

*Note: I would advise against writing 'We All Now Know' on your white boards and definitely resist labelling your low ability learner as a child 'Regularly Underachieving National Targets.' Their parents won't like it.

The moment you realise it's
the first Monday back...

YOUR PRESENCE IS REQUIRED!

Someone wiser than me, once said that,

"whatever begins as voluntary in schools, soon becomes mandatory."

That one off event you planned because you had time and were interested, quickly becomes annual, requiring unquestioned participation...

When I was a lad, teachers enjoyed their job. Back then, children were allowed to be children, rather than workers in a statistics factory.

Grandpa was known for his tall tales, but this one was just unbelievable...

18

A Midsummer Term's Dream

Scene One: A school staffroom.

Cakes, sweets, sugar saturated hot drinks, chocolate and diet books litter the coffee tables as a group of female teachers discuss the day. A single handsome male teacher sits quietly in the corner, doodling absently.

Teacher 1 : (bursts in excitedly) Oooh! Oooh! Did you hear the fireman is in today for this years fire safety training?

Teacher 2: Mmm, lovely. Something nice to look at for a change!

Teacher 3: Hey! Hey! I'd slide down his pole!

Teacher 4: Hey! Hey! I'd polish his helmet!

Teacher 5: Hey! Hey! I hope he shows me his hose!!

Bawdy laughter follows. Then teacher 6 comes in looking forlorn.

Teacher 6: Aww. You won't believe it girls. It's not a fireman. They've sent a bloody woman this year...

(All the female teachers tut and sigh dramatically.)

Male Teacher: A firewoman? Oh I might go and check her out...

Teacher 1: Typical bloke.

Teacher 2: Disgusting.

Teacher 3: You know, that's just SO disrespectful to women...

20

SAVE THE TEACHER!

This once abundant creature is suffering a severe drop in numbers. Healthy and competent teachers are being driven out of their natural habitat by parasites, (inspectors) and predators, (bad headteachers).

A young female teacher, captured by night vision at 2 a.m. She forages through old books for valuable resources that she will need to survive in this hostile and unforgiving environment. Many, (40%), don't survive...

"Miss, what will you do tonight when you get in?"
"Oh, probably read a book or something..."
BRING ME WINE !

*And to try a positive spin....

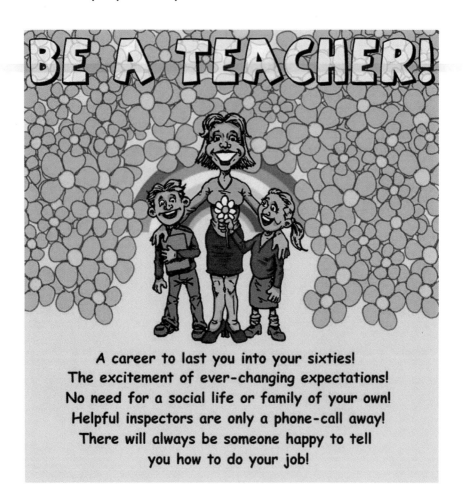

*Nah. It's not working!

Even Bigger Brother

THE GENESIS OF SCHOOL INSPECTORS

Legend has it, that on a dark and wind tossed night, as the lightning slashed the murky clouds above, an unholy creation crawled into the world. With a cry of anguish, the first school inspector was born. The creature was the the illegitimate offspring of a drunk traffic warden and a blind driving test examiner who'd lowered his standards one Christmas. The creature soon discovered that in conditions of paranoia and fear, it could thrive and by sucking the life out of teaching staff, soon rapidly reproduced in number.

Some people dispute this tale and offer an alternative one that Ofsted was created to root out poor teaching and to make schools better. However, this is surely less believable, as we apparently STILL have failing schools and teachers. If Ofsted had been any use, surely by now they would have completely eradicated bad practice?

It would appear then, that the actual continual existence of Ofsted, is evidence of its own failure.

Nah! The first story is far more believable...

The Viking Ancestry of School Inspectors

'I love this job Sven. Even though the monks live in constant fear of us, they still go to pieces when we arrive. They will do ANYTHING to make us leave happily!'

Those Who Can't... Inspect

Once the school inspectors, headteachers or self important educational advisors have ripped into a lesson, using their impressive wisdom and colossal experience, it is strange they don't then choose to demonstrate **how it should be done...**

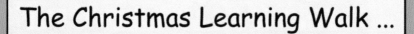

Ofsted Almighty

'Our Inspector, who art in classroom,

Ofsted be thy name...'

It is with an almost religious reverence, that the school inspector is treated. When they descend from the 'Heavens' , golden clip board tucked under angelic arm, headteachers all but prostrate themselves in front of them.

The WORD of OFSTED is translated by the divinely chosen priests (headteachers) for the benefit of the great unwashed masses, (the staff).

In another alarming similarity, the WORD of OFSTED is often used to justify all sorts of atrocities, that, to be fair, the Mighty Ones themselves probably never intended...

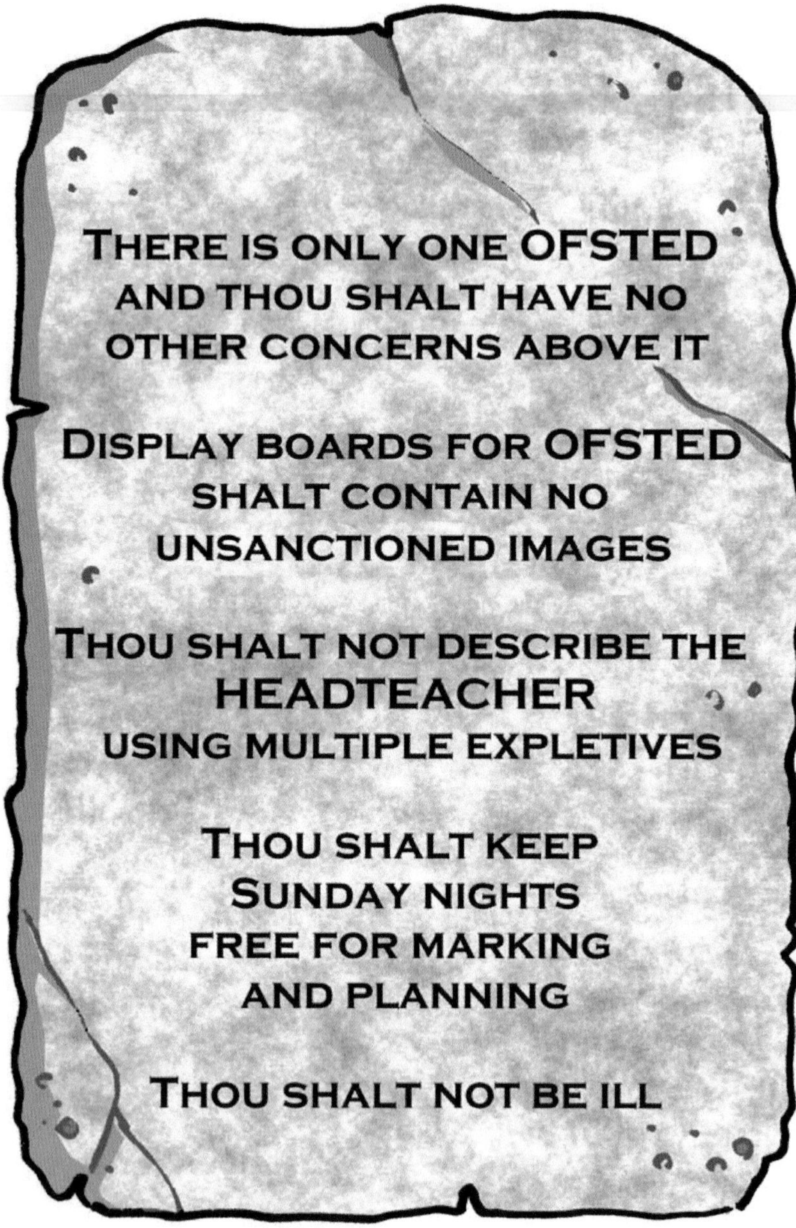

THERE IS ONLY ONE OFSTED
AND THOU SHALT HAVE NO
OTHER CONCERNS ABOVE IT

DISPLAY BOARDS FOR OFSTED
SHALT CONTAIN NO
UNSANCTIONED IMAGES

THOU SHALT NOT DESCRIBE THE
HEADTEACHER
USING MULTIPLE EXPLETIVES

THOU SHALT KEEP
SUNDAY NIGHTS
FREE FOR MARKING
AND PLANNING

THOU SHALT NOT BE ILL

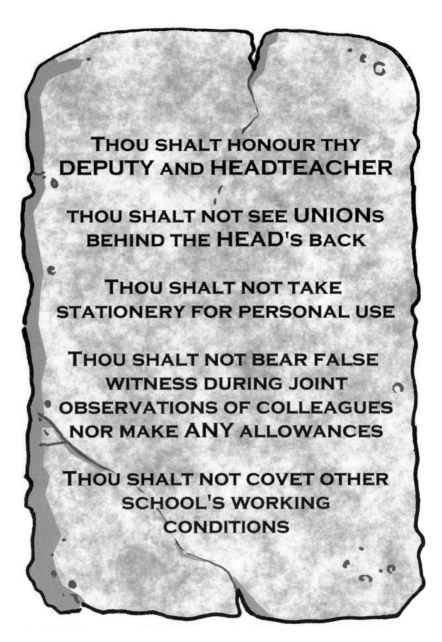

THOU SHALT HONOUR THY
DEPUTY AND HEADTEACHER

THOU SHALT NOT SEE UNIONS
BEHIND THE HEAD'S BACK

THOU SHALT NOT TAKE
STATIONERY FOR PERSONAL USE

THOU SHALT NOT BEAR FALSE
WITNESS DURING JOINT
OBSERVATIONS OF COLLEAGUES
NOR MAKE ANY ALLOWANCES

THOU SHALT NOT COVET OTHER
SCHOOL'S WORKING
CONDITIONS

35

The Viking Ancestry of School Inspectors (2)

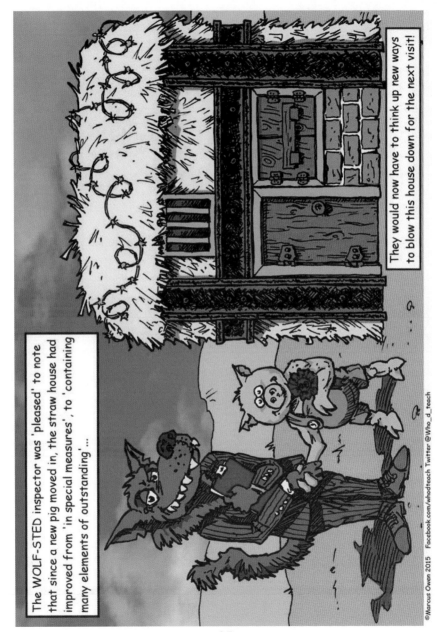

The WOLF-STED inspector was 'pleased' to note that since a new pig moved in, the straw house had improved from 'in special measures', to 'containing many elements of outstanding' ...

They would now have to think up new ways to blow this house down for the next visit!

©Marcus Owen 2015   Facebook.com/whodteach Twitter @Who_d_teach

37

Empty Heads

41

On becoming an academy,
the headteacher said that there
would be hardly any changes...

43

THE BAD SCHOOL HANDBOOK

'Sneaky Meeting Tricks'

If you have a staff meeting or training day, always state it will finish half an hour past when you think it will. This isn't to allow for unpredictable events, but rather to allow you to appear both generous and to swindle the staff out of a break at the same time.

Bear with me.

Start the meeting with apologies for it likely over-running, but point to the break time you've timetabled in and say if everyone works through break, we may just finish early.

Everyone will agree in order to escape the tedium and so you can eliminate the break time, finish when you wanted to and appear like you are on the side of the poor working saps!

Nyah ha ha ha ha!

Miss Pelling: "Headteacher, that stick the government sent you is non-statutory. You don't HAVE to hit the staff with it!"
Headteacher: "Nyah ha ha! Just try and stop me!"

Hammering successful staff with continuous observations, is like taking your car back to the garage after it has passed its M.O.T.
It says more about the kind of 'driver' you are, than the quality of the car!

Gimme More More More!

"It's just one more little job. It should only take a few minutes..."

This is the common excuse given as trivial, distracting and time consuming tasks are added to an already bulging workload. Form filling, box ticking, stamping charts, collecting stickers, three stars and infinite wishes etc etc etc.

The idea is to try and suggest this won't detract from the job of actually teaching children, (which is really why you are there after all...) , or far less importantly, affect your quality of life at home. What escapes notice is that all these harmless '*few minutes*' are accumulative and soon add up to hours of extra time.

But what kind of 'unprofessional' would argue about a little job that only takes a few minutes eh?

THE BAD SCHOOL HANDBOOK

'De-skilling to Dismissing'

Headteacher, do you have a pesky experienced teacher who may know more than you? Maybe this person has a history of good results, a bank of reusable resources and a team of supportive colleagues. Maybe they have the respect of the staff and their opinion carries weight, even when it disagrees with yours. But how to rid yourself of this troublesome but effective teacher?

Just DE-SKILL them to pull that rug from under their feet and make them vulnerable to criticism. Make their method of working 'illegal' within your school. Say it's outdated and unproductive. (Just ignore their results). Introduce your own methods and make sure you patrol the building to enforce them. Move this trouble-maker to a different year group or subject they have little experience in. Perhaps make them work with people you know they don't get on with or even better, in complete isolation. Maybe even pass them up a class of children with fake results and impossible targets.

Before you know it, that member of staff will be open to all sorts of unfair observations and if you withdraw all support, you could probably even squeeze them out completely! Retirement or resignation here we come!

The Season of Good Will

We trained hard... but it seemed every time we were beginning to form up into teams we were reorganised. I was to learn later in life that we tend to meet any situation by reorganising, and what a wonderful method it can be for creating the illusion of progress while producing confusion, inefficiency and demoralisation.

Previously attributed to Gaius Petronius A.D.66

It may not be Roman, but it's still a great quote!

53

Testing

1,2,3...

If teachers Sub-levelled their washing...

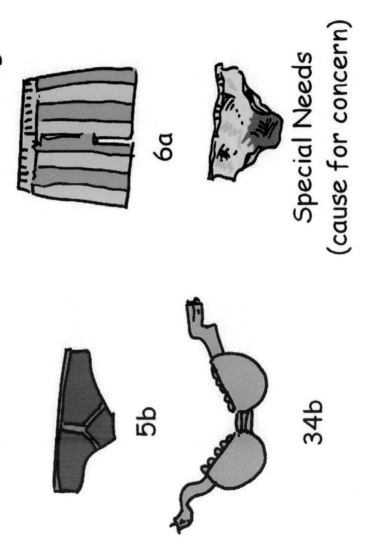

6a

Special Needs
(cause for concern)

5b

34b

Cycling

Tests

1. The head feels pressurised by the new tests she has to have administered, so she talks to the staff.

2. The staff now feel pressurised by the new tests they have to work towards, so they talk to the children.

3. The children now feel pressurised by the new tests they have to do, so they talk to their parents.

4. The parents feel now pressurised by the new tests they have to support, so they talk to their government.

5. The government now feels pressured about the tests they have brought in, so they make brand new tests and then talk to the heads again.

6. Go back to 1.

A favourite mark-book doodle...

'I can confidently say my maths set are all 4Bs. Their names? Haven't got a clue.'

63

'Your baby is doing fine, we just have to do a few tests. It's nothing serious. We just need to take some blood samples, check her hearing and assess her basic numeracy and literacy skills.'

THE FUTURE?

Angels

and

Demons...

Playtime?

THE FINGER OF DEATH

In handling disruptive children, you can set up sticker charts, initiate conduct management routines and even constantly negotiate terms for not being a pain in the backside. However, one really effective weapon from the teacher arsenal, next to sarcasm and tucked just behind the disapproving 'tuts', is the *finger of death*.

Just pointing a rigid finger at a naughty child, whilst saying nothing, can have amazing results, if performed correctly. Once this technique is mastered, the raised voice will hardly ever be needed again.

I first saw this method deployed effectively when I was a newly qualified teacher. Jackie was an expert in the field, who could paralyse a child with one extended digit, backed up only by a steely gaze. The bravest child would soon crumble without a word being said. Continual pointing could often bring confessions and an eruption of apologies. The range of the 'finger of death' was impressive. Experts like Jackie could cover a whole playground without breaking a sweat.

Zoology of the School Thug.

Observations of a Young Teacher

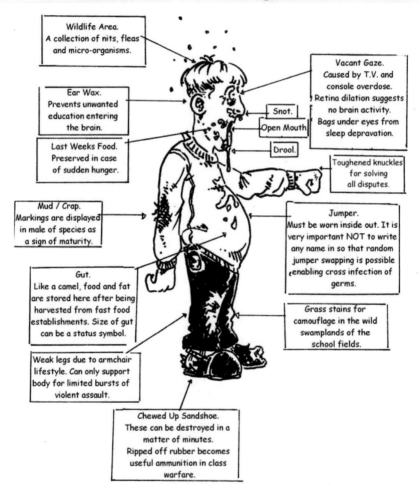

Wildlife Area.
A collection of nits, fleas and micro-organisms.

Ear Wax.
Prevents unwanted education entering the brain.

Last Weeks Food.
Preserved in case of sudden hunger.

Vacant Gaze.
Caused by T.V. and console overdose. Retina dilation suggests no brain activity. Bags under eyes from sleep depravation.

Snot.

Open Mouth

Drool.

Toughened knuckles for solving all disputes.

Mud / Crap.
Markings are displayed in male of species as a sign of maturity.

Jumper.
Must be worn inside out. It is very important NOT to write any name in so that random jumper swapping is possible enabling cross infection of germs.

Gut.
Like a camel, food and fat are stored here after being harvested from fast food establishments. Size of gut can be a status symbol.

Grass stains for camouflage in the wild swamplands of the school fields.

Weak legs due to armchair lifestyle. Can only support body for limited bursts of violent assault.

Chewed Up Sandshoe.
These can be destroyed in a matter of minutes. Ripped off rubber becomes useful ammunition in class warfare.

*Note : This only applies to the sub-species of the school thug. Parents of nice children need not be offended. (Unless they really want to be...)

72

VISITING SPEAKERS

Someone relatively unused to public speaking in schools, marks the success of their visit by how much noise they can get the children to make.

Usual activities include lots of standing up and sitting down in a confined space, screaming out answers and of course the old 'I can't hear you?' line.

Once the crescendo has peaked, the visitors are then all too happy to hand back hysterical whooping children to their teachers who will then have to assume the villainous role of *'miserable sod'* in order to get any kind of work done.

Miss Brown was forced to consider whether overusing the positive reinforcement policy had any adverse effects...

From the Mouths of Babes...

A Lesson

In Politics

"You know, I 've always liked you teachers..."

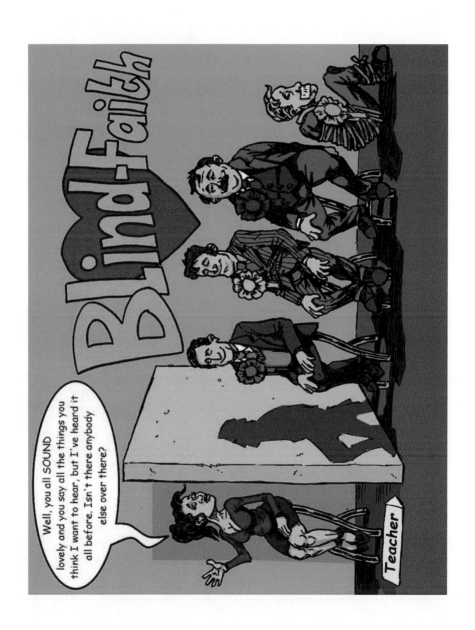

82

* Yes, I know it's different for Scotland... but R.I.P. English, Welsh and Northern Irish Education isn't quite as snappy!

The
Home
Front

89

And what have you been playing at today?
Are you an artist, a musician, a sports coach, an accountant, a priest, a police woman or even some kind of nurse?

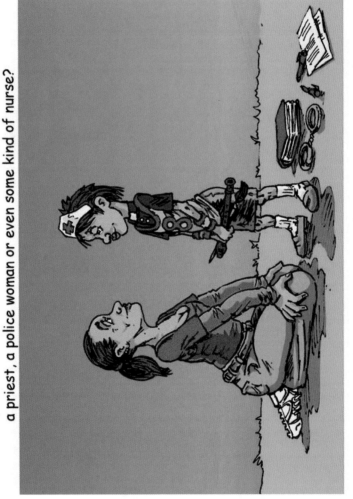

Don't be silly Mummy, I am just playing at being my teacher...

SCHOOL TRIP TROUBLE

The school couldn't afford to fund the trip on its own, but after most parents agreed to contribute, it had been planned. Then one parent 'kicked off' about having to pay for a school trip. She had made a strong and verbally colourful argument that as they had two children in the year group, they couldn't afford to pay for the *'effing'* bus and *'effing'* museum admission twice over. The family could afford to all go abroad every year, but that was obviously *'effing'* essential...

Barraged by swear words and wagging fingers, the headteacher had to make a difficult snap decision and 'remembered' / invented a school policy about waiving fees for siblings. despite the family committing to pay before the trip was even booked, Other, less aggressive families were made to keep to their promise to share funding.

However on the day of school trip, the two brothers marched swiftly over to the museum gift shop, smirking at their class while waving their impressive spending money in front of the other kids, Their poor classmates were understandably annoyed that the two lads, who had been bragging about getting in for free, now had funds for pencil sharpeners and novelty pencil cases.

Things were getting heated, the two boys about to be lynched by the mob, until a quick-witted teacher snatched the money away and immediately 'remembered' / invented a school policy for not buying souvenirs during school trips!

Apparently it wasn't *'effing' fair...*

*I'm with the parent here!

WANDERERS RIGHTS

People who want all children to have unrestricted and unarguable access to toilet breaks are indeed championing the basic human right to 'extract the urine.'

HomeWork

It's strange that some of the busiest of parents seem to be the ones who demand the most homework set for their kids. I would have thought, given their lifestyle, they would find it difficult to devote extra hours to sitting with their child and supporting them with some school set task.

The alternative would be to send the child to their room for long periods and not be able to see them all evening...

Oh... right...

Oi Teacher! As long as I can think of anyone who has a worse job than you and as long as I can totally misunderstand your actual working hours, you'll get no sympathy from me mate!

^Thankfully a minority in my experience!

RAYS
OF
SUNSHINE

It's not all bad of course. The theme of my books is whinging because teachers like to whinge and we have a lot to whinge about. However, there are many lovely unexpected pleasures that can make the day so much more bearable...

When the class nuisance is unexpectedly absent.

When the assembly goes on for far too long.

When you get a last minute cancellation on parent's evening and actually leave early.

When some brave soul dares to extend playtime beyond its official duration.

When your own method of explaining succeeds where the new school approved version does not.

When staff meetings are cancelled.

When a parent or child thanks you and means it.

When a child is proud of their work, no matter what anyone else would think.

When a class leaves you, still talking about the lesson as they go home.

One personal favourite moment was the morning I pointed out a brilliant winter sunrise to a passing register monitor. We watched the lazy sun's rays spread across frosty roof tops, through a canopy of lavender and peach clouds.

This was nothing to do with targets or levels or planning or observation. I had no idea of the child's previous history in sky-gazing or what her targets were for 'aesthetic response to nature.'

The moment was simply making a child aware of something wonderful, noticing an opportunity for education and responding to it.

Moments like this are when you can understand why you <u>would</u> want to be a teacher...

About The Author

Marcus Owen survived 20 years as a class teacher and is still able to communicate on most days. Although his sense of humour was often brutally attacked, he remains able to draw the odd amusing cartoon.

Marcus has produced three books now, 'Who'd Be A Teacher?', the original collection of sketches, 'Don't Do What The Dodo Does!', a rhyming child safety book and now, 'Who'd Be A Teacher? - Colourful Language'. (Released in black and white as 'Seeing it in Black and White')

He is British, six foot tall and enjoys jellied sweets.

He has met loads of lovely parents, loads of lovely children and a few nice headteachers. But they aren't what his books are about.

He has met no nice school inspectors, traffic wardens or speed camera operatives.

Find him on Facebook.com/whodteach

Email :whod_be_a_teacher@hotmail.com

Who'd Be a Teacher Indeed?

I was warned of course, by a retired teacher, the father of my earliest childhood friend.

"You're going to teach? You must be mad!" Trevor roared, in his usual jovial good manner, *"They are ruining teaching you know!"*

I didn't listen. I was only 19, just leaving for college and so of course knew far better. For a long while, I really thought I had mastered it too. I was soon a successful teacher, allegedly a natural, according to the wonderful pair of ladies who mentored me in those first embryonic years. I had firm classroom control, good subject knowledge, strong relationships with parents and even managed a sense of humour on some days! I went from full contracts to supply and back again, getting a real feel for the different schools in my local area. I even took on teaching assistant work on occasion. As a secret teacher, I observed both fantastic and shocking practice from the sidelines. This forever gave me sympathy and respect for our over-worked and under paid T.A.s.

Eventually, responsibility beckoned and to pay for a mortgage, I settled down in one school for about 10 years. There was something comfortable about becoming part of the nearby community, knowing some lovely families, growing closer to comrades in arms and fine-tuning my teaching through years of practice. It would be unfair to discuss specific experiences from that period, but of course, like any job, there were both good and bad.

Nationally, however, the British government's attitude to teaching was becoming almost exclusively negative. The desperate search to find a scapegoat for society's failings was coming to focus on education again. It was a probably considered a good vote catcher.

"Hey parents! Your kids are doing badly at school, but it's nothing to do with them, you, their background or constant government interference. It's those awful teachers! Lets go get them!"

Like a horror movie mob of villagers, the government began circling teachers with metaphorical pitch forks and burning torches. The Witch Finder General, Secretary for Education, Mr. Michael Gove, lead the assault, armed with an almost comical misunderstanding of what education was, accompanied by an infinite arsenal of personally developed and approved innovations. Headteachers literally cowered in fear of the Ofsted inspection goons, who would descend like Monty Python's Spanish Inquisition, seemingly creating failure criteria on the spot. Again, this would be funny if not for the awful pressures it exerted upon teachers, whose only crime was to try their best to help other people's kids. Inspections and league tables created statistic-driven schools that squashed children into numbers and hammered teachers into submissive automatons, expected to deliver the curriculum in uniform manner, regardless of personal approach.

Then they started on our pensions. An intrinsic part of the deal we signed up for, was no longer safe. Schools were being pushed into becoming academies and any contract those teachers thought they had, was apparently no longer valid. Monitoring staff's work-life balance became simply an unexplored option to many headteachers. And morale, well, that didn't really matter did it? Completely non-statutory extra classroom observations were being dressed up in all kind of fancy new names and presented as useful. They certainly weren't useful to the many teachers reduced to nervous wrecks before, during and after self-appointed experts gave out their clipboard-informed pearls of wisdom, reflecting whatever current theory of education was fashionable at the time. This hysteria was infecting all the schools and even the Unions were struggling to cope with the constant attacks upon teacher's professionalism. Union suggestions for working to contract were undermined and discouraged, making it almost distasteful to do so in many schools. It's sad to note that all this was made possible in schools by the collaboration of many in senior leadership structures, more bothered about school reputation and their own climb up the career ladder, than the welfare of staff and students. Education had begun to really stink.

My outlet was my art. Being art trained, I had always doodled when my mind wasn't being particularly engaged. I was unusually productive during staff meetings and training days. I was able to both listen and draw, so it made an often dull experience far more enjoyable. As the national onslaught upon teaching began to increase, so the subject matter of my cartoons began to focus more upon what was annoying me about modern schools. It helped me to laugh at it, but only for a while.

Finally I'd had enough. I quit the job, for many of the above reasons but also due to some personal issues that made continuing as a teacher too difficult. It was not a decision I took lightly, with a young family to support and no real safety net beneath me. I just knew I could no longer stomach what was happening and it certainly wasn't going to improve. The effect it was having on me was not worth it. Four years of teacher training and twenty years of experience in numerous schools seemed pointless. Like many who dared to make the 'Great Escape' from teaching, I was now faced with what to do next.

After a while I began to realise many of my cartoons may appeal to others like me, who were also disillusioned with the profession. I collected many of my doodles together, redrew some, spoke to other teachers for inspiration and then created many more. I put these into a book package and released it on Amazon as my first book, '*Who'd Be A Teacher?*' The title was a question many teachers seemed to continually ask. The book illustrated different topics such as work-life balance, school inspectors, bad head teachers and questionable practices, all drawn in black and white pen and ink, just as I had originally done. I used **Facebook** and **Twitter** to promote the book myself, creating new colour work for the digital world and managed to reach hundreds of thousands of people.

The most regular question I receive is whether anyone I've known throughout my career is represented within the book. The answer is no. I honestly think it would be terribly unfair to show ex-colleagues in a comical light, even those I didn't especially like, (to put it mildly!). Also, caricature takes a long time to do and I would rather make up my own unique characters. Sometimes elements of people have sneaked in from my subconscious mind. My late father seems to have elbowed his way into one picture for example, but I know he wouldn't mind.

Am I done with teaching? I honestly don't know. I didn't quit because I wasn't good at it and I am somewhat loathe to waste the skills I have developed, but in its current state, the classroom is not a place I want to be for long periods. Equally, the publicity I alone can give my work won't generate enough sales to keep me in chocolate biscuits forever. But should one of those publishing houses want to snap up exclusive rights to my books, I doubt I would have to think about that decision for too long.

Also available by the same author:

13613693R10067

Printed in Great Britain
by Amazon.co.uk, Ltd.,
Marston Gate.